Projects Inspired by the Olympics

Rebecca Bruce, Rebecca Carnihan, Sarah Deas, Flora Ellis, Céline George, Sue Reed, Ceri Shahrokshahi, Claire Tinker and Liz Webster

Acknowledgements

Liz Webster and Sue Reed (chapter 1) would like to thank all the members of Aldingbourne's art club, who produced the fantastic artwork. A big thank you to Mrs Davies and Mrs Herbert for their hard work and dedication in helping us create such fabulous displays. It was a real team effort.

Céline George and Rebecca Bruce (pages 18–19) would like to thank the Year 6 children at Hilden Grange School for their striking artwork.

Flora Ellis (pages 20–21 and 26–27) would like to thank Mike Pudifoot, Moira Cooper and all of the children at Sherbourne Primary School who were involved in the project. A big thank you to Alison Sage for her valuable support.

Ceri Shahrokshahi (pages 22–23) is grateful to the children in Year 3 for their hard work, enthusiasm and input. And a big thanks to Anora Ahad and Carol Whitehead for keeping me on track with the project.

Sarah Deas (pages 24–25 and 28–29) would like to thank Miss Mary Caveney and Ms Emma Condon for their help as well as the children in reception class at John Betts Primary School for their enthusiasm and wonderful artwork.

Rebecca Carnihan (chapter 3 and page 13) would like to thank Executive Headteacher Mrs Cynthia Eubank, Head of School Ms Carol Wilson, and especially the junior children of Grinling Gibbons Primary School in Deptford, London for their hard work, enthusiasm and for truly 'going for gold' when making the work for this book.

Claire Tinker (chapter 4) would like to thank the wonderfully creative children at Dore Primary School and their Headteacher, Mrs Sue Hopkinson. As always, thank you to my very encouraging and supportive family and friends.

Published by Collins
An imprint of HarperCollins*Publishers*
77–85 Fulham Palace Road
Hammersmith
London
W6 8JB

© HarperCollins*Publishers* Limited 2012

10 9 8 7 6 5 4 3 2 1

ISBN-13 978 0 00 745564 5

MIX
Paper from
responsible sources
FSC
www.fsc.org FSC® C007454

Rebecca Bruce, Rebecca Carnihan, Sarah Deas, Flora Ellis, Céline George, Sue Reed, Ceri Shahrokshahi, Claire Tinker and Liz Webster assert their moral rights to be identified as the authors of this work

British Library Cataloguing in Publication Data
A Catalogue record for this publication is available from the British Library

Cover design by Mount Deluxe
Internal design by Lodestone Publishing Limited
Photography by Elmcroft Studios
Edited by Alison Sage
Proofread by Gaynor Spry

Printed and bound by Printing Express Limited, Hong Kong

Browse the complete Collins catalogue at
www.collinseducation.com

Techniques: collage (pages 12, 14, 26, 29, 30, 42, 43 and 44); costume making (page 37); digital design work (pages 21 and 46); drawing (pages 6, 8, 10, 14, 17, 18, 22, 23, 28, 40, 44, 45 and 47); marbling (page 40); model making (pages 13, 17, 20, 22, 27, 28, 30, 34, 35, 41 and 46); painting (pages 8, 23, 32, 34, 35, 41, 42, 43, 44, 45 and 48); photo art (pages 8 and 30); printing (pages 21, 32, 36, 40 and 42); sculpture (pages 7 and 23).

Contents

Introduction

The modern Olympic Games was created to give the countries of the world a chance to celebrate achievement in friendship, to compete without war. It is also a rich source of topics across the curriculum that stimulates learning in a creative way.

We've aimed to provide a programme of imaginative and achievable ideas to explore the Olympics through activities and displays. If children are involved and enthusiastic, they will take pride in working together and they will take pleasure in learning.

Each project begins with a whole-class introduction, usually with stimulating and relevant material from the internet and other sources. This is followed by a practical activity, which might involve drawing, painting, collage, printing, sculpture and 3D modelling, costume making, model-making or marbling. It may also include relevant games and there are suggestions for cross-curricular work so that each activity becomes the basis for a larger piece of work.

Chapter one sets the scene for the Olympics and is designed to help children understand the history of the Games and its relevance to us today.

Chapter two shows how much planning and preparation goes into any major event, from designing buildings right down to the production of posters and tickets. What would a big event mean to a child's town or village? How could they be involved?

Chapter three explores how to celebrate – in art, drama and literature, including many inventive ideas, such as continent costumes and opening ceremony displays.

Chapter four discusses the games themselves and how individual sports can be celebrated visually.

All of the projects were carried out with a particular age group, but can be adapted for use either with older or younger children. For example, the Legacy display (page 28) was created by 4- and 5-year-olds, but could easily explore the lasting effect of a big event with children at the top of the school.

Finally, it is important to stress that all of the projects can and should be adapted to suit a teacher's own particular requirements. We've suggested ways to develop and extend the original ideas to make an integrated plan of work for a term, or you can simply dip into the book to find ideas to complement existing projects.

For busy teachers, the projects are intended as a starting point and an inspiration to form the cornerstone of many successful activities, and we hope you enjoy celebrating the Olympics with your class, as much as we have!

Rebecca Bruce,
Rebecca Carnihan,
Sarah Deas, Flora Ellis,
Céline George, Sue Reed,
Ceri Shahrokshahi,
Claire Tinker and
Liz Webster

5

History

The Glorious Greeks

Introduce the children to the Ancient Greeks, to set the scene prior to learning about the Olympics.

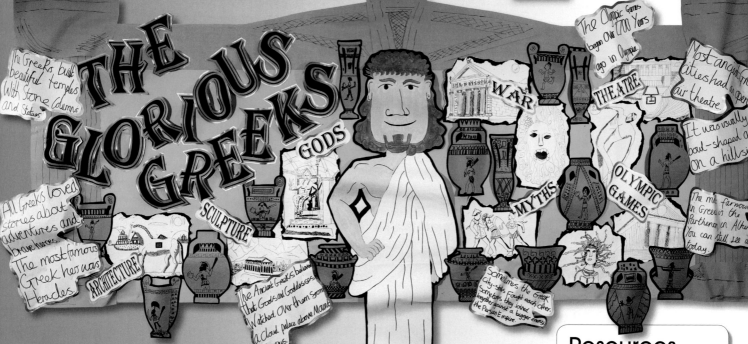

Approach

1. Teacher arrives in role of an archaeologist; s/he has discovered some incredible artefacts dating back to the time of the Ancient Greeks. S/he splits the children into groups and gives them a box of 'artefacts' to unveil (pictures, models of Greek vases, temples, clothes, etc). The children must decide what these artefacts tell them about Ancient Greek civilisation. One of the artefacts should reveal that sport was important in Ancient Greek times. The 'archaeologist' then talks through each artefact, describing life in Ancient Greece and explaining that the Greeks had a sporting festival, called the Olympics.

2. Give each child a paddle with the word TRUE on one side and the word FALSE on the other. Using an interactive whiteboard, show children statements about the Ancient Greeks, including the Olympics. The children must decide if the statements are true or false.

Resources

- Ancient Greek images for inspiration
- Paddles with TRUE on one side and FALSE on the other
- Interactive whiteboard
- Pencils, black ink pens, felt-tips
- Orange paper for the stone/wooden temple
- Orange card for the pots
- Blue backing paper and white paper for the extra drawings and information
- Computer and sheets of gold and orange paper (for the lettering)
- PVA glue

3   **Greek temple:** pin blue backing paper on a display board to create the sky.

4   Draw a temple framing the display onto orange paper. Create a stone effect with black ink pen. Cut out and fix on the wall.

5   Draw and collage a large Ancient Greek figure for the centre of the display.

6   Children make pen and ink drawings of Ancient Greek images.

7   **Greek pots:** after looking at examples, ask children to draw and cut out 2D pots from orange card. Create a pattern of figures in the Greek style on each pot.

8   Children write facts about the Ancient Greek civilisation and add these to the display.

9   **Lettering:** make letters on a computer and print on orange paper. Stick onto gold backing paper and cut out each letter. Use a Greek-style font.

10 Add key words relating to Ancient Greeks.

Clay masks: give children a tile-shaped piece of clay (see page 23). Using clay tools create a face mask, emphasising features such as eyes, mouth, hair, etc.

Resources
- Clay
- Clay tools

Cross-curricular links

Literacy: using the words 'Ancient Greeks', write an acrostic poem.

A Gallery of Gods

This section introduces children to the Greek gods and goddesses.

Approach

1   Teacher in role of Hermes visits the class wearing a set of wings and drops off a package. Whilst running through the classroom, Hermes explains that he cannot stop because he has other messages to deliver. The teacher arrives and opens the package to find objects and information relating to one of the gods. Teacher reads the information and invites one of the children to wear/hold the props. Hermes returns again and again until the class has learnt about several more of the gods. Finally, Hermes leaves clues about Heracles, son of Zeus, and the teacher tells the children the myth of how he created the Olympics.

2   **Gallery of gods:** decide who to include in your gallery. Draw around several children in appropriate poses.

3   In groups, cut out, paint and collage each image to transform it into one of the Greek gods. Using a photo of themselves, and printing out to the correct size from a computer, children can add their own faces to the figures.

4   **Lettering:** make letters in a Greek-style font, (see page 7). Cut out and back with gold paper.

5   Cut out white clouds from paper and fix around the gods to create a heavenly effect. Add written questions and facts about Greek gods and assemble on a blue background.

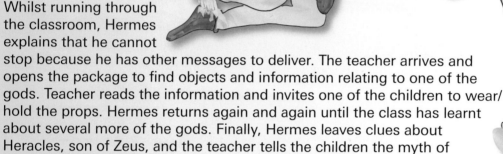

Resources
- Images of Greek gods for inspiration
- Large sheets of white paper, pencils, paint
- Felt-tips and markers to draw around children.
- Scissors, PVA glue and recyclable materials for collage
- Gold paper (to back the lettering)
- Pale-blue backing paper

6   Children should draw and paint pictures of Greek gods to add to the display.

The Greek Alphabet

Introduce the class to the Greek alphabet.

Resources

- Cardboard and pieces of card
- White, yellow and black paint and brushes
- PVA glue
- Blue backing paper
- Gold paper and computer for lettering

THE GREEK ALPHABET

The Greek Alphabet is a set of 24 letters.

It is the first and oldest alphabet.

Greek letters are pronounced differently to English letters.

It has been used since the 9th century.

Can you use the Greek alphabet to write your name?

It is still in use today.

Can you find out what these Greek symbols mean?

Approach

1 Cut mosaic tiles roughly 2cm square out of cardboard, and paint them white, black and yellow.

2 Give each child a rectangle of card and help them create a border with the yellow tiles. Glue in position. Now ask children to pick a letter from the Greek alphabet and cut and assemble the black and white tiles into that shape. (It helps to draw it out first!)

3 Glue the tiles in position and display all the cards in a block with gold lettering and interesting facts about the alphabet on blue backing paper. Extend the task by asking children to spell their names, improvising where letters are missing. Other children can then work out which word spells which child's name.

Cross-curricular links

Literacy: investigate how the word 'alphabet' was formed.

Literacy: ask the children where else they might have come across the Ancient Greeks?

Once Upon a Time Olympics

This section focuses on how the Olympic Games began and how they have developed over time.

Approach

1 Mind map with the children what they already know about the Olympics. Teacher records in large Olympic rings any facts past or present about this wonderful event.

2 Tell the story of the Olympic Games to the class from the distant past to the present day. Play 'Mix and match'. Show groups of children a selection of pictures of events in the history of the Olympics and ask them to place them in the correct order. This could be organised as a mini-race. You could extend this activity by removing a picture and asking the children to identify what is missing.

Resources
- Research including images that tell the story of the Olympics
- Blue (backing paper), gold, orange, green, black and white paper
- Chalk pastels and fixative, pencils and felt-tips
- Laurel leaf shapes
- PVA glue

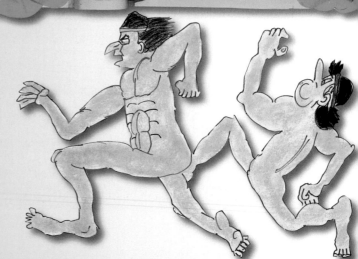

3 **Timeline:** create a giant, timeline display telling the story of the Olympics, called Once Upon a Time Olympics. Make the title out of gold paper, printed in a Greek-style font and back each letter onto a laurel wreath shape.

4 Instruct the children to draw and chalk pastel pictures and images that tell the story. For example, Zeus could begin the story as the Olympics were founded in his honour. Talk through the ideas and images with the children first to help them with their drawings.

5 Make captions on the computer, using a Greek-style font.

6 To make the display, back the pictures and place on a blue background together with the captions. Add laurel leaves cut out from green paper among the pictures for effect.

Cross-curricular links

History: play 'Run for a Ring'. Make two large sets of Olympic rings and place on a board. Make a set of cards with questions about the Ancient Olympics and a set with corresponding answers. Split the children into two teams and lay out the answer cards at the other end of the room. The teacher reads out a question and a child from each team must run to collect the correct answer card. The first child to collect the card can place it in one of their Olympic hoops. The team that collects the most cards is the winner.

P.E.: organise a mini Ancient Olympic Games.

Get Into Shape

In this section, the children will create a mathematics display focusing on 2D shapes.

Approach

1 Collect and draw different mathematical shapes. Explain that the ancient Greeks were mathematicians and some words we use today (geometry, pentagon) come from Greek.

2 Look at pictures of athletes and their equipment, and talk about what shapes their bodies make when they are in action.

3 Using stick-on shapes, ask children to assemble different Olympic athletes in sporting poses. Stick these on backing paper and cut them out.

4 Ask children to write about their shapes on the computer and to print these out in a suitable font.

5 Use a suitable font and print lettering for the title. Cut out and assemble on a display board covered with backing paper.

6 Assemble the display together with the shape athletes and any key words you have discussed.

Resources
- Researched images of athletes
- Coloured, stick-on geometric shapes
- Yellow and black backing paper
- White paper and computer

The Olympic Stadium

Take inspiration from some of the stadiums built in the recent past. The 1976 Montreal stadium could suggest an alien, a spaceship, or even an armadillo. And the 2008 Beijing stadium is now known as the Bird's Nest because of its woven, lattice-like structure. Giving children a choice of different materials to construct their roofs makes for contrasting results and gives them a chance to use problem-solving skills.

Approach

1 **Stadium track:** use a paper plate for the base of the stadium. (If your plate is flimsy, glue two plates together.) Paint the top with sienna and once this is dry, cut a rectangle of green fabric or paper and glue this onto the plate. When dry, draw running-track lines around the green fabric in white pencil.

2 **Stadium wall:** cut a length of card at least 6cm in height to overlap around the plate. To make a stadium entrance, cut the length slightly shorter than the plate circumference.

3 Using sienna and white paint, mix different shades for skin tones. Create audience faces with a series of fingerprints in rows, changing the shade several times. Allow to dry.

4 Curl the perimeter wall around the track and stick the meeting edges together with sticky tape. Put a drizzle of PVA glue where the perimeter wall meets the track, and allow to dry.

5 **Stadium roof:** let each child choose a different material, e.g. lolly sticks, pipe cleaners, etc. They should then work out how to construct and attach a roof for their stadium. Bird's Nest effect is achieved by hole-punching the wall and threading string back and forth to create a geometric design. Card and lolly sticks are glued, and held in place with masking tape (removed once glue is dry).

Resources
- Large strong paper plates
- Sienna and white poster paints
- Green fabric or paper
- White pencils
- White or patterned flexible card
- Sticky tape
- Pipe cleaners, lolly sticks, string, etc
- PVA glue
- Hole-punch (adult use only)
- Masking tape

Cross-curricular links

Geography: research the different countries that have held the Olympic Games.

Literacy: the words 'Olympic' and 'stadium' have a Greek origin. Research other words with a Greek origin.

The Wall of Fame

This section encourages children to focus on Olympian stars, exploring different ways to present them.

Approach

1. Discuss with the children what makes a great Olympian. Think of what words to use, e.g. determination, commitment, dedication, self-belief, ability.

2. Explain that today the class are going to learn about people who have changed the face of the Games. Using a PowerPoint presentation, display several great Olympians in action and tell their story.

3. **Wall of Fame:** create a wall effect using a large sponge dipped in brick-coloured paint and printed on creamy-brown paper. This makes a great background to display children's work.

4. **Lettering:** using ICT write the title in a brick pattern and print. Back on red paper and mount.

Resources

- Computer and PowerPoint presentation on Olympians
- Sponge, brick-coloured paint and creamy-brown backing paper
- Brick pattern printed from the computer (for the lettering)
- Coloured pencils and felt-tips
- Gold corrugated card
- Images from the internet, magazines, gold paper and scissors
- Selection of patterned, black, white and coloured paper for collage and backing children's work and mounting letters
- PVA glue

Cross-curricular links

Literacy: write a biography of a great Olympian.

P.S.H.E.: ask children to think of five things they are good at, or five things that make them who they are. The children could either write or draw pictures to illustrate.

5 **Portraits:** children draw observational portraits of great Olympians of their choice. Frame the pictures with corrugated gold card and attach to the Wall of Fame.

6 Children should label their chosen athletes and write or print important facts they have discovered about them. Cut out this information, back it on gold paper and add to the Wall.

7 **Key words:** remind children of the qualities they identified for an Olympic athlete. Print out these key words, cut them out, back and display them.

8 **Photo collage:** ask children to cut out of magazines or print images of their favourite Olympic stars from the internet. Collage these images splinter-fashion on gold paper, cut out and add to the Wall.

9 **Sporting equipment collage:** using drawings of objects related to different Olympic sports, ask children to create an athlete in action. Back on black paper and add to the display.

10 **Olympic rings:** discuss with children how they recognise different sports and sporting equipment. Ask them to use simple black paper shapes to collage an athlete in action on a coloured Olympic ring.

11 **Patterned collage:** using plain and patterned paper in simple shapes, collage an Olympic athlete. Back all work, cut out and attach to the display.

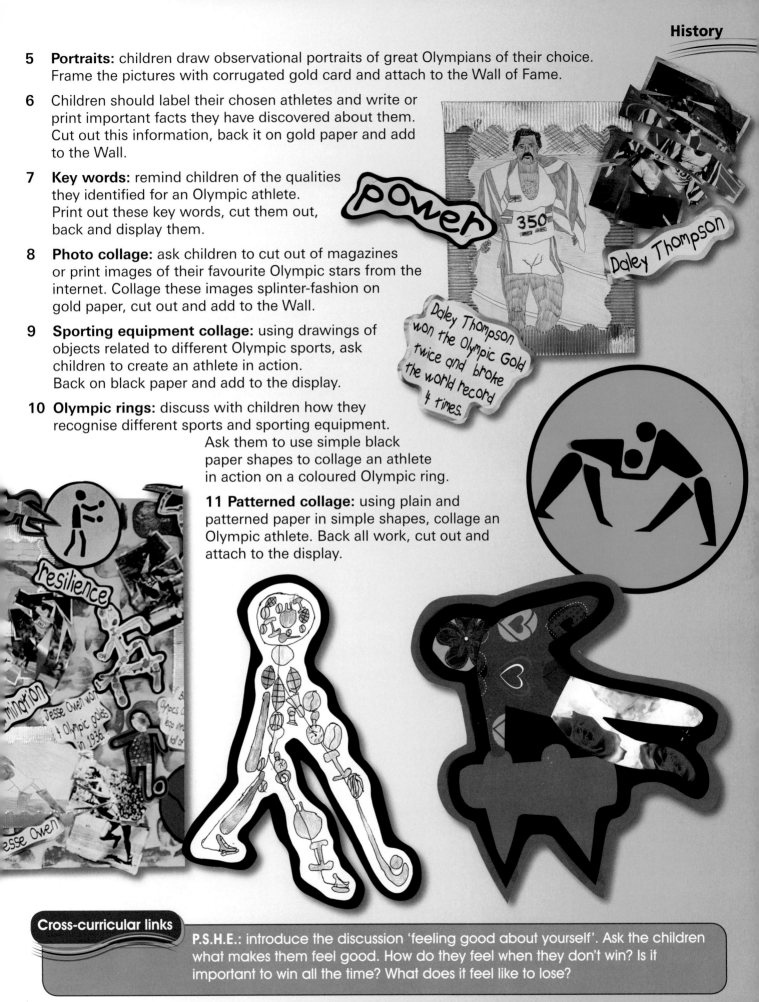

power

Daley Thompson

Daley Thompson won the Olympic Gold twice and broke the world record 4 times.

resilience

Jesse Owen won 4 Olympic golds in 1936

Jesse Owen

Cross-curricular links

P.S.H.E.: introduce the discussion 'feeling good about yourself'. Ask the children what makes them feel good. How do they feel when they don't win? Is it important to win all the time? What does it feel like to lose?

Record Breakers

Ask the children what it means to break a record.

Resources

- Pictures of athletes
- White, red, silver and black paper
- Silver pen
- Camera
- PVA glue
- Card
- Gold paint and brushes

Approach

1 Teacher selects a child to carry out a challenge, e.g. how many bean bags can you balance on your head? etc. Choose an activity that is fun and not too serious. The teacher times the event. Then other children are picked to see who can do it faster. Once a child has succeeded, the teacher explains that a record has been broken; not a world record or an Olympic record, but a class record.

2 Choose more fun challenges so that several children have a chance to be record breakers. Take photos.

3 Show images of athletes and ask children to guess if they are record breakers or not. Each time, the teacher explains what the athlete did in fact achieve, telling their stories, e.g. Jesse Owen, Zola Budd, Kelly Holmes, Usain Bolt, Steve Redgrave.

4 Create a chequerboard with black and white backing paper.

5 Make lots of circles of black stiff paper, and draw circles on them in silver pen to give the 'record' effect. Add circles of plain paper for the middles. Attach to the display.

6 Make the title 'Record Breakers' out of big red printed letters stuck onto the records.

7 Back photographs of children breaking class records on red paper, and add these to the display. Make these a selection of fun challenges. Include printed captions backed on silver paper, explaining what each child has achieved.

8 Cut out a big circle in card and glue on extra scraps of card in layers to create a 3D effect. Paint gold. Arrange these oversize medals on the display.

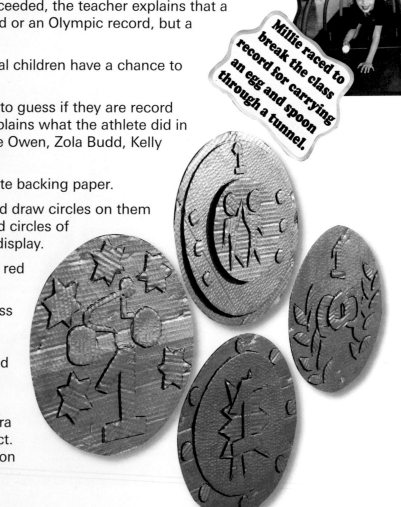

Cubist Olympic Athlete

Approach

1. Use cubism for inspiration to create an Olympic athlete. Each child cuts out a cube shape from a template. Illustrate with a pictures of body parts using oil pastels. One body part (such as a foot) should be drawn on each face of the cube.

2. Glue the cube together.

3. Arrange the cubes to create an athlete.

4. Print out key words you have discussed about athletes, back and stick onto the athlete.

5. Add any other equipment made out of cardboard. This athlete is a weight-lifter.

Resources
- Cardboard and scissors
- Oil pastels
- PVA glue
- Computer and paper

Cross-curricular links

Maths: using the most up-to-date *Guinness Book of Records*, ask children to look up various records, both silly and sensible.

Maths: ask the children what they can discover about a cube.

P.E.: ask the children to create a dance exploring their feelings about winning and losing. What movements show celebration?

The Architect's Vision

An architect's job is to design buildings which enhance the lives of people who use them; they should be fit for purpose, practical, light and spacious, beautiful, and durable. Structures designed for the 2012 Olympics ought to convey the spirit of the Olympics and people should enjoy using them both in the short term and in the future. Point out to children that drawing is an important tool in the design process, and encourage them to focus on simplicity. As the architect, Mies van der Rohe, famously said, 'Less is more.'

Resources

- Mind maps
- Sketch books
- Pencils
- Images of landmark buildings including the Aquatic Centre 2012 by Zaha Hadid and the Velodrome by Hopkins Architects

Approach

1 Look carefully at a selection of images of iconic landmark buildings, discussing what materials have been used, and how sustainable they are.

2 Talk about the purpose of a building and how its design can echo its use.

3 Discuss how architects use shape and form to design buildings.

4 Using a mind map, encourage the children to explore their ideas.

5 Ask children to choose a building and make a detailed pencil sketch of all or part of it.

6 They should write the name of the building next to the sketch.

Mind Map: Olympic Buildings

Legacy
What will happen to it after the Olympics?

Landscaping
Will there be sculpture/planting/street furniture?

Sustainability
How does it affect the environment?

Scale
How big is it?

NAME OF STRUCTURE

Materials
What are the main building materials? Why?

Inspiration
What is it inspired by?

Visuals
What is the shape, texture, colour and pattern?

Cross-curricular links

Literacy: ask the children to describe a building that interests them and explain why.

History: ask the children to research the history of their favourite sport. How did it start?

Create large chalk pastel designs of buildings linked to the Olympic theme. The designs should include basic shapes reflecting the sports to which each building relates. You can also use shapes from the Olympic logo or the traditional Olympic ring design.

Approach

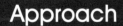

1   Look at a selection of basic shapes and ask the children to draw them in their sketch books using shading to create a 3D effect.

2   Tell the children that they will be designing an Olympic structure which will echo the use of the building.

3   Encourage them to design their stadium structure by building up a combination of 3D shapes in white pastel on black paper.

4   Suggest the children add some landscaping details to put the stadium in its setting.

5   Show them how to shade the stadium shapes with white pastels.

6   Ask children to add figures in the foreground to convey scale.

7   Display on coloured backing paper and decorate with sporting imagery.

Resources
- Sketch books
- Collection of basic 3D shapes
- A3 black paper
- Pencils and rubbers
- Soft pale-coloured chalk pastels
- Coloured backing paper

Cross-curricular links

Geography: research some of the ways people choose to build their homes across the world.

Welcome to Our Games

Ask children to invent their ideal Olympics. What will they call it?

Big competitions need a lot of planning. Discuss how you will look after the athletes. What will they need?

And how will you look after the people who come to watch? They will need tickets and programmes. Make a life-size kiosk where children can give away leaflets and 'sell' tickets.

Posters are a good way to tell everyone about your Olympics. What should they say? How should they look?

Approach

1 **Kiosk:** cut the top and bottom flaps off two cardboard boxes, and the top flaps off the remaining box. Assemble so that the top box is upside down, with its bottom forming the top of your kiosk.

2 Draw a large rectangle in the top box with marker pen. This will be the 'window'. (A child can check this is at the right height by standing next to the boxes.)

3 Cut out the rectangle and also the backs off all the boxes (adults only). Tape the boxes together firmly with masking tape.

4 Make a cardboard shelf by folding back tabs on two sides of a piece of cardboard, to make a square the same size as the inside of the kiosk. Tape the tabs firmly inside the kiosk on either side, just below the window.

5 Now paint your kiosk to match the colour theme for your Games!

Resources
- Three large cardboard boxes, at least 50cm high
- Masking tape (which can be painted)
- Scissors
- Poster paint and marker pen

20

Tickets and Advertising

Use an ICT programme to create tickets, programmes and advertising leaflets. Children can design them in their chosen colour scheme, experimenting with different fonts and layouts. Think about ways to encourage people to come to the Games, such as special offers on seat prices. Another important way of advertising your Games is to design a poster.

Approach

1 **Poster:** a good poster catches the eye. Show children some iconic poster art, especially from the Mexico 64, Tokyo 68 and Moscow 80 Games. These designs were bold and used strong, geometric shapes. Encourage children to choose three or four simple shapes to make their poster design. Sketch this out in sketch books.

2 Draw each shape onto sponge or packing foam and cut out with scissors. (You could also use polyboard. See page 33.)

3 Demonstrate how to print. Pour paint into a tray, and dip in a shape, covering it evenly with paint. Print one colour at a time, leaving the poster to dry before printing a different colour. Remember to start with the palest colours and build up.

Resources
- Posters of past Olympic Games
- Sketch books and pencils
- Sponge/ packing foam
- Three or four different colours of liquid poster paint
- Painting trays/ plates

Cross-curricular links

Literacy: explore how advertisers use persuasive techniques to promote their products.

Maths: look at ticket prices for the 2012 events. How much will the tickets be to the school's Games? How much discount could be offered to senior citizens, children, groups?

Geography: which countries have hosted the Games in summer and which in winter? Why is that? Use atlases or globes to locate the countries.

The Olympics in Your Town

Ask the children to imagine what would happen if the Olympics took place in their town.

How would they welcome the athletes? And what would they tell visitors about their area?

Resources

- Interactive white board
- Aerial maps of your area
- Website links to city council sports grounds, etc.
- Paper, paints, felt-tips
- Card, range of craft materials, PVA glue, scissors

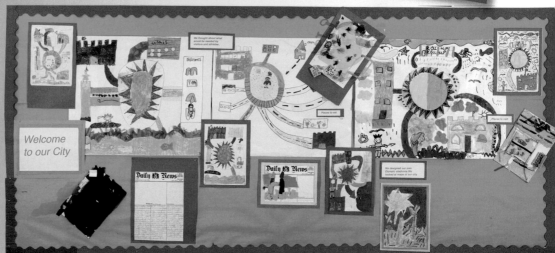

Approach

1   **The Olympics in our town:** research cities where the Olympics have been held, looking at images. Now look at maps of your local area. Discuss with children where a large event like the Olympic Games could take place, and draw up a list of questions. How would visitors get there? Where would they live? Where will they eat? What else will they need? What would they like to do to relax?

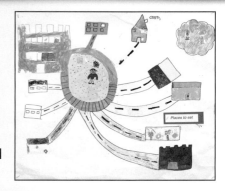

2   Interview or write to a city councillor or to the director of a sports centre to ask for their views on what the Olympics might mean for the area. Write a report of what they say.

3   Each child should draw a bird's-eye-view of the Olympic stadium and village. Colour with paint and felt-tips. Display together with children's written work.

4   **3D model:** make a 3D model of the Olympic village. Discuss with them what they want to include and each child can design and 'build' with scraps (paper, wire, feathers, etc) and PVA glue on a piece of card.

Cross-curricular links

Geography: why and how do towns change? What makes them grow? What makes them shrink?

Literacy: start a school magazine, including articles, photographs, and news of school activities. It could also be uploaded to the school website.

Music: write a song to welcome visitors and competitors to the town.

An Olympic Souvenir

Look at artwork commissioned for the Olympics. A special way to greet visitors to your school would be a welcome mosaic made from things in the school environment, using ideas from the artist Andy Goldsworthy.

Approach

1 **Mosaic drawings:** let each child choose something in the school environment – plants, leaves, tree bark, soil, rubbings of brick, playground surface, etc, and sketch a design. Draw and colour the designs and display.

2 **Tiles:** talk about ways to fit a design onto a clay tile shape. Each child transfers their design onto tile-shaped slices of clay, sculpting it with clay tools.

3 Seal with PVA glue (see page 34) and paint when dry.

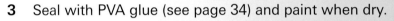

We collected things that grow in our outdoor spaces,

We made our design from clay,and painted them.

We drew still lives and looked at colours.

Resources
- Paper, pencils, oil pastels, coloured pencils
- Clay, clay tools
- PVA glue, paint, brushes

Cross-curricular links

P.S.H.E.: you can extend the project by helping children to design a souvenir pack for visitors, which shows how their town is unique.

P.E.: children could also choreograph and perform a welcome dance to show what there is to celebrate about their home city.

23

Sportswear

Encourage children to think about their own bodies when they exercise. What changes do they notice? Discuss the effect of exercise on our breathing and heart rate. When we exercise, we get hot. Ask the children why we wear sports clothes. We need to wear P.E. kit for sports as we want our uniform to stay 'fresh'. Show images of athletes wearing clothes specific to a particular sport and discuss why they are suitable. Ask the children to choose a famous athlete to base their figure and sportswear on.

Children will make a fully-articulated athlete, 30cm high, and design sports clothes, suitable for the athlete's chosen sport.

Approach

1   **Articulated athlete:** ask children to draw around pre-drawn and cut templates for the separate body parts: a body, head and neck, forearm, upper arm, hand, thigh, lower leg and feet.

2   Colour in the separate pieces with a skin tone crayon appropriate for their chosen athlete and cut out the separate pieces. Draw on a face and add wool hair.

3   Mark each piece to show where the limbs will be attached and punch a single hole through the card.

4   Attach the limbs of the athlete by overlapping the card holes and fixing with a split pin so that each body piece can be moved separately.

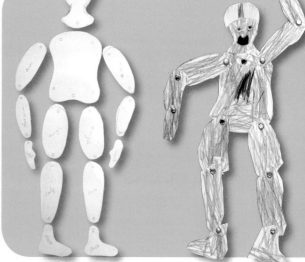

5   Depending on their athlete's sport, children can choose which clothes and fabric would be most successful. Explore and test a range of different fabrics. Ask the children if they think it would be comfortable to wear a denim swimming costume or a waterproof vest for running? Show the children a selection of clothing templates. (Older children will want to make their own!)

6   Demonstrate to children how to check that the clothing templates are the right size for their athlete. Then they can draw around these onto their chosen material. (Don't make them too tight!) Cut out the shapes.

7   **Make a sandwich:** back of clothing, then the athlete, then front of clothing. Stick the clothes together down the seams with PVA glue. Take care not to get any glue on the athlete or the parts won't move.

Resources
- Card
- Card templates for articulated athlete
- Pencils
- Single hole punch (adult use only)
- Split pins
- Range of skin tone crayons
- Card templates for sports clothing (front and back)
- Scraps of different fabrics and wool
- Scissors
- PVA glue and spreaders

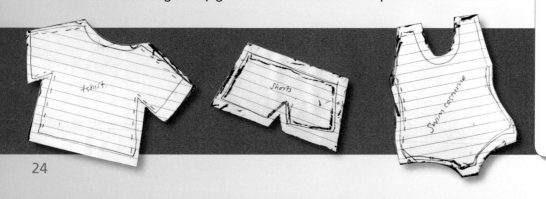

8   Now make each athlete
    pose, demonstrating a
    sport. Children can use
    the athletes in an Olympic
    Park small world role-play
    area, as part of a table top
    display, or fixed to a wall
    display. They could even be
    suspended from the ceiling.

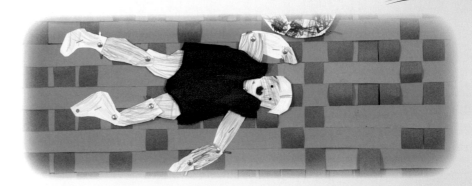

Literacy: write a play using articulated athletes in small world situations.

P.S.H.E.: each country has a distinctive design and colour for their athletes' clothes.
Discuss how far uniform is important in creating a sense of identity and belonging.

Science: design an investigation to find out which is the best insulator: cotton
or polyester.

How do Athletes Train?

What would an athlete's diary look like? How do they train? What do they eat?

Different sports demand different training routines and each athlete trains in a special way. Encourage children to research the life of their favourite athlete to discover what makes it so interesting.

Choose two athletes and show how their training and diet varies – often dramatically – before a major competition.

Resources

- Felt and fabric scraps
- PVA glue
- Scissors
- Sugar paper
- Card and felt-tips
- Researched photos, drawings and text

Approach

1 **Athletes:** show the children images of athletes and let them choose two contrasting sports (e.g. long distance runner and high jumper). Draw outlines of two bodies onto stiff card, around 75cm high. Cut out the bodies separately.

2 Cover each card body with skin-coloured felt and stick down with PVA glue. Add details to the faces with felt-tips. From fabric scraps, cut out clothing shapes and glue them in place (see page 24). You can make any special equipment out of card, e.g. a swimmer might have goggles.

3 **Diary:** for the background, use coloured sugar paper the same size as your display board and draw two parallel curved paths from top left to bottom left. Divide the curved paths into sections representing the weeks and months leading up to a big event. Use different colours for each month.

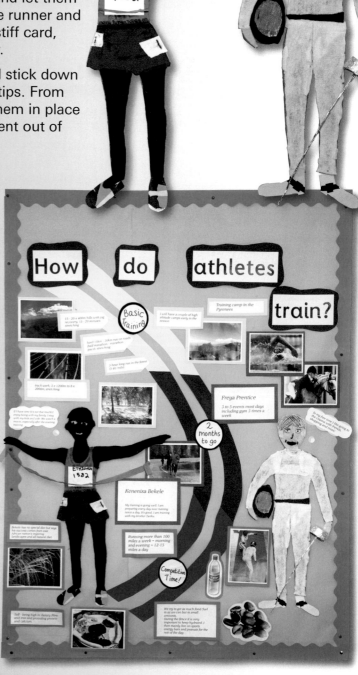

4 Attach one athlete on each side of the calendar path, together with their equipment.

5 Help children to research their chosen athlete's training in the run-up to a big competition and attach photos, drawings and text along the path.

Olympic Fuel

What makes up a balanced meal? Explain to the children about different food groups, so they understand why top athletes need to eat particular foods. Children should explore what different foods give us and how to combine them to make an appetising meal.

Resources

- Sketch books, pencils
- Air-drying clay
- Acrylic paints
- PVA glue and paper plates
- Paper labels

Approach

1 **Clay meal:** research which foods provide a balanced meal. Next, sketch out your favourite balanced meal onto paper.

2 Using air-drying clay, mould the shapes of the food.

3 Paint the food, arrange on a paper plate and glue in position.

4 Label the foods by food group, explaining what they do for us. Display next to the diary so that each athlete can have their own meals!

Cross-curricular links

Science: investigate what sugar does to our bodies and our teeth.

Maths: make graphs/charts showing what different foods contain.

Literacy: research Beth Tweddle and the demands of becoming an athlete. Would it be worth it?

Olympic Legacy

Introduce the concept of legacy as something left at the end of a special event which will be remembered and enjoyed. What do children think could be the legacy of the Olympics? Think about **place** (London), **pride** (teamwork, reaching goals, new friendships around the world), **healthy living** (food, exercise), **sustainability** (environment/recycling) and **buildings** (venues re-used after Olympics). Create Olympic legacy mobiles as a memory time-capsule of the Games. These will hang in front of a London skyline display (the **place** aspect of the Olympic legacy).

Approach

1 **London skyline:** as a class, decide between a day or nighttime setting. Cover a display board with pale blue or black backing paper.

2 Show children a map/image of the River Thames and draw the river onto the backing paper. Children can now add their own collaged detail, e.g. tissue paper for the river, fluffy summer clouds, or glittery stars.

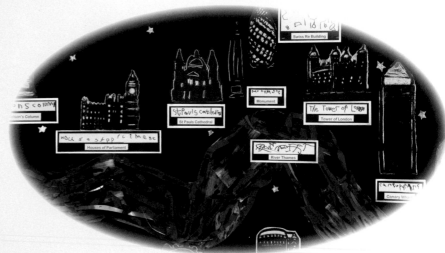

3   Show images of London skylines and point out famous landmarks, e.g. the London Eye, Big Ben, Tower Bridge, The Shard, Wembley Stadium, etc. Encourage children to choose a building and draw it onto coloured sugar paper. They can either draw silhouettes outlined with white pastels for night, or coloured pastels for a daytime panorama.

4   Cut around the buildings and stick them onto the display.

5   **Mobile:** in groups, bind two garden canes firmly together with string in an 'X' shape. Attach a loop of string at the centre of the X to hang up the mobile. Next make some cards to depict each legacy.

6   **Card legacies:** discuss why people feel **pride**. Ask the children in each group to draw a design on a square piece of card to show their feelings of pride about the Olympics. Ideas of items to draw include flags, concertina people (friends from around the world), a favourite athlete or event.

7   Stick collage materials onto the card design with PVA glue. Allow to dry and cut out.

8   Repeat steps 6 and 7 for the other three legacy headings. Ideas of items to draw include:
    Healthy Living: running shoes, bicycle, fruit and vegetables, bottle of water, bed (getting enough sleep), shower/bath/basin (washing ourselves)
    Sustainability: footprints painted green, recycling dustbin
    Buildings: Olympic Stadium, Aquatics Centre, Velodrome.

9   Give each child a length of ribbon. Staple four card legacy designs to the ribbon at regular intervals, starting from the bottom and working upwards.

10 Tie each of the four ribbons to the X shape and hang the finished mobile in front of the London skyline.

Resources

- A3 coloured sugar paper
- Map of the River Thames, pictures of London skylines
- Pastels
- Scissors
- Garden canes (each approx. 30cm)
- Strong string
- Coloured ribbons (one per child)
- Card squares 10cm by 10cm (four per child)
- Pencils
- PVA glue
- Collage materials: tissue paper, glitter, beads and sequins
- Stapler

Cross-curricular links

History: research the lives of people who have left a legacy in the fields of music, science and literature.

Celebrations

Opening Ceremony Diorama

Inspire your group by showing them images of past Olympic opening ceremonies. Many take place at night and a dark background will highlight the great bursts of colour you can bring to the project. Select a limited range of colours (as pictured) for a strong impact or use a mixture of colours for more subtle effects. This is scaled-down costume design and there is a lot of scope for some inventive performing outfits.

Children can now 'perform' the opening ceremony. You could even add lighting!

Approach

1   **Stage:** make the structure by cutting off the side of the box to reveal an open stage. Draw a large curve on the top of the box sweeping from the front left corner to the front right corner. An adult should now cut this out with a knife.

2   **Fireworks:** cut metallic paper into strips. Add twists by curling around a pencil and glue the strips together at the centre to make a starburst. Glue these onto the top half of the black paper. (Measure to check that the paper fits along the curve in the top of the box.) Cut out small flags and glue below the fireworks.

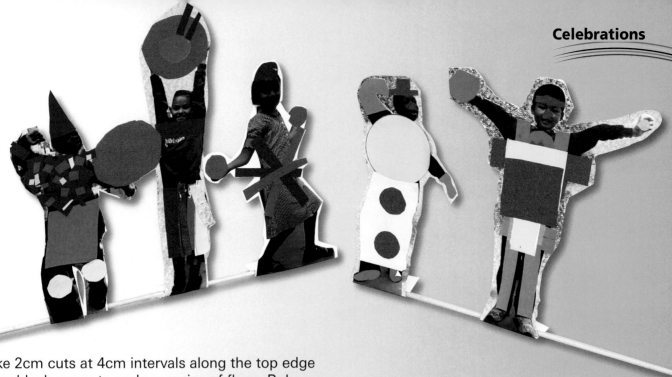

3   Make 2cm cuts at 4cm intervals along the top edge of the black paper to make a series of flaps. Rub glue along the curve of the box, and bend each flap back. Press flaps onto the gluey surface of the box and allow to dry.

4   **Figures:** photograph the children singly or in pairs, posing as if performing in the opening ceremony. They may choose sporty or dance poses. Print on A4 paper in black and white and cut out. Now draw simple shapes (circles, squares) on coloured paper and assemble them on the photos to make imaginative costumes! Stick figures onto sparkly or flexible card and cut out, leaving a 0.5cm edging, and a flap at the bottom to bend and glue into position.

5   Add an Olympic flame to your diorama, held by one of the figures.

6   **To perform:** select a couple of figures and glue onto a stick. (An adult can use a glue gun for quick results – or use PVA leaving the figures face down while the stick bonds to the figure.) The figures can now be pushed across the front of the diorama to 'perform'.

7   This diorama can be made with mixed ability/age groups and adapted as necessary.

Resources

- Images of Olympic opening ceremonies
- A large cardboard box
- Sheet of flexible card
- Large sheet of black sugar paper
- Glue sticks
- Digital camera
- Coloured paper
- Metallic paper
- Small flags (research on internet)
- Wooden stick
- Craft knife (adult use only)
- Pencil

Cross-curricular links

Geography: what do flags represent?

P.S.H.E.: research different kinds of celebrations and festivals around the world.

Friends From Across the Seas

This project looks at the culture of different countries around the world. Each child explores a country of their choice and some children may choose to research their heritage countries. Good sources are folk art, textiles, monuments, etc., found in libraries and on the internet. The World Art Map pictured here has 22 artworks and is 2m wide, but it could be made any size to suit the display area.

Approach

1 **Map:** take two A2 sheets of paper and sticky tape together to form a rectangle almost as big as a standard display board. With a group of children paint the entire surface with blue poster or acrylic paints. Encourage children to create different shades for their ocean by adding white to lighten, and green to make turquoise, etc.

2 The next stage may best be done by an adult. Draw a map of the world on an A1 sheet of stiff paper/card. Draw freehand, or attach card to a whiteboard, and trace a projected image of a world map.

3 Select images from your source material (e.g. Taj Mahal for India) and draw a small picture of each image onto A4 paper. Add colour using paint or colour pencils. Allow to dry, cut out the image and glue onto the map. Glue the map flat onto the ocean with PVA glue, using a glue gun for a quick bond (adult use only).

4 **World art:** using a sharp pencil, draw another image from your researched material onto a polyboard tile. If the group are new to block printing, begin with a demonstration (see page 36, step 3). Print onto A4 white card/paper.

5 Once the prints are dry, trim to equal size squares, and mount, evenly spaced, on four strips of white paper or card. Finally, attach the four strips of artwork as a frame for the blue ocean panel, tucking them behind the map for neatness, and pin into position on a large display board.

Resources
- Poster or acrylic paints
- Block printing inks
- Polyboard tiles 21cm × 21cm (or smaller)
- Pencils
- Four sheets of A2 stiff white paper/card, two sheets A1
- A4 white flexible card or paper
- Trays
- Rollers
- PVA glue and gluesticks
- Water colours or colour pencils
- Sticky tape

Cross-curricular links

Geography: ask the children to research climate across the world, looking at the physical geography of the children's chosen countries.

P.S.H.E.: research the number of languages spoken by children and staff at your school.

History: research the story of migration across the world.

Medals

An Olympic event isn't complete without medals! Encourage the children to think about which sport they want to choose and begin this project by making designs on paper. Other sources of inspiration could be your local area, school or town, e.g. an historical figure or monument.
To extend the project, the children could photograph one another in different sporty poses, or try some figurative drawing before the designs take shape.

 This activity involves using Plaster of Paris. Children must be carefully supervised when they use it.

Approach

1 **Medal mould:** soften Plasticine in your hand, form into a ball and place on the card or tray. Using fingers and thumbs make the ball into a bowl with a flat base.

2 Make impressions in the Plasticine with lolly sticks, etc. to create your design. (Remember letters or numbers will come out backwards!) Take care not to make any holes and fill any cracks with spare Plasticine.

3 Take a length of ribbon, cross over the two cut ends at right angles and staple together.

4 **Plaster:** fill a container three-quarters full with water and add spoonfuls of Plaster of Paris without stirring until a peak of powder appears at the surface of the water. Stir slowly until the mixture resembles single cream. Pour immediately into the mould(s).

5 Place the ribbon ends deep into the liquid plaster, at the top edge of the mould. The plaster should cure (set) within minutes. This is an interesting process for children to see. Allow to set for at least a day (or when it no longer feels damp) before peeling off the Plasticine mould. Do this slowly and carefully, to minimise loss of detail. It will come off most easily in a warm room or on a warm day.

6 The surface of the medal must be sealed before painting. Mix PVA glue with water, brush the thin white mixture over your medal and allow to dry. Now you can paint your medal gold, silver or bronze!

Resources
- Plasticine
- Modelling tools, lolly sticks, matchsticks, scrap card, plastic trays
- Metallic paints – gold, silver and bronze (or copper) and brushes
- Containers
- Plaster of Paris
- PVA glue
- Ribbon lengths approx.1m long
- Stapler (adult use)

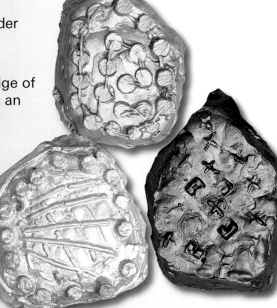

Cross-curricular links

History: research the history of money and coins.
Science: research liquids, solids and gases.
Literacy: describe a win by a famous Olympic sportsperson against the odds.

Trophies

Show children images of different Olympic sports events, pointing out the sculptural qualities of the athletes' physical movements and even their sports equipment. Look at different sports trophies and trophies in general. The children's trophies can even be made for your school Sports Day, becoming a real design brief for a real event.

Approach

1   Choose recyclable materials to build your trophy. These could be a paper plate for the base, a water bottle for the stem and a balloon for the cup or ball shape.

2   Inflate a balloon to the desired size and knot tightly to stop it going down. For a near spherical ball put the knotted end of the balloon into the cut plastic bottle. To make a semi-circle cup shape, put the rounded end of the balloon into the cut bottle with the knot at the top.

3   Fix your chosen plate, plastic bottle, sticks, etc. into position with the balloon, using sticky tape. (Children can take turns helping the person next to them.)

4   Cut Modroc into strips 6cm wide. Show children how to use Modroc: dip once into water, allowing excess water to run off and massage to soften. Then start at the bottom of the trophy, covering the plate and bottle stem first. Use no more than two layers of Modroc to cover the balloon.

5   Allow at least one day to set hard, and remove the balloon if possible, trimming the edges of the cup with large scissors and shaking off any excess bits.

6   Mix a little PVA glue with water and brush over the surface of the trophy. Allow to dry. Now paint, using two or three metallic colours to make an interesting mixture of tones and a fine brush for detailed areas. Trophies needn't all be gold!

Resources

- Images of Olympic sports events and trophies
- Balloons
- Small plastic drink bottles, cut in half to remove the neck
- Paper plates
- Sticky tape
- Sticks and other junk materials
- Modroc
- Water and containers
- PVA glue
- Bronze, copper, gold, silver metallic paints
- Brushes

Cross-curricular links

Science: research the concept of evolution. How do animals compete?

P.S.H.E.: ask the children to write about something that made them feel very proud.

35

Celebrating People of the World

This project is based on the iconic Olympic rings, designed in 1912 by Baron Pierre de Coubertin, founder of the modern Olympic Games. These coloured rings represent the five continents of Europe, Africa, the Americas, Australasia and Asia. The children will enjoy researching art from each continent, using this to inspire the images they print.

Approach

1   **Map:** this stage is best done by an adult. Draw each of the five continents freehand on large separate sheets of flexible card, simplifying each one. (You could also attach the card to a whiteboard, and trace a projected image.) Lightly draw horizontal guidelines across each continent for the prints to be applied.

2   **Block printing:** using a sharp pencil draw an image on a polyboard tile to represent one of the continents: e.g. for Australia, a kangaroo, or Sydney Opera House, or indigenous Australian art (as seen here).

3   If the group are new to block printing, demonstrate first:
Squeeze a length of printing ink from the tube into the top end of the tray.
Dip the roller lightly into the ink, leaving most of it, and roll the roller up and down in the tray until you hear a 'sticky' sound. Once the roller is evenly covered, roll it over the polyboard tile so it, too, is evenly covered.
Pick up the tile, turn it over and place on the map, pressing down evenly with the flat of your hand. Carefully lift the tile to reveal the image.
Reapply the ink and repeat the process. The prints will soon partially dry, and you can then apply a darker colour over some of them for a richer effect.

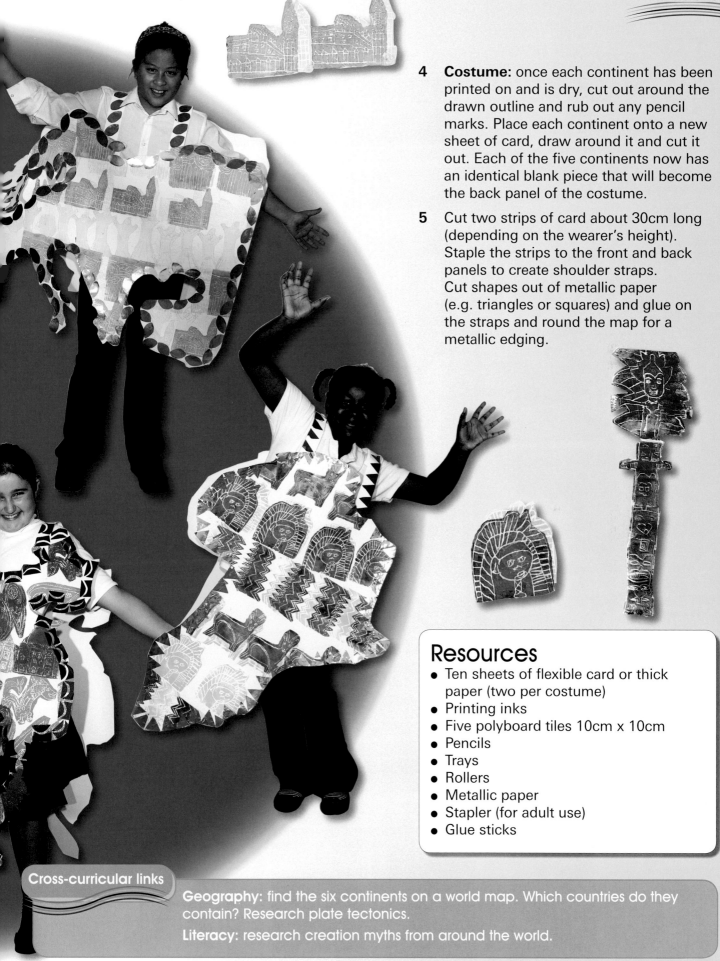

4 **Costume:** once each continent has been printed on and is dry, cut out around the drawn outline and rub out any pencil marks. Place each continent onto a new sheet of card, draw around it and cut it out. Each of the five continents now has an identical blank piece that will become the back panel of the costume.

5 Cut two strips of card about 30cm long (depending on the wearer's height). Staple the strips to the front and back panels to create shoulder straps. Cut shapes out of metallic paper (e.g. triangles or squares) and glue on the straps and round the map for a metallic edging.

Resources
- Ten sheets of flexible card or thick paper (two per costume)
- Printing inks
- Five polyboard tiles 10cm x 10cm
- Pencils
- Trays
- Rollers
- Metallic paper
- Stapler (for adult use)
- Glue sticks

Cross-curricular links

Geography: find the six continents on a world map. Which countries do they contain? Research plate tectonics.

Literacy: research creation myths from around the world.

All Sports Pictograms

The International Olympic Committee (IOC) decided on 26 sports for the 2012 Summer Olympic Games. The very first Olympic Games had just one running race, for men only. Throughout its history, the number of events has constantly changed and in 1900, women took part for the first time – but only in tennis and golf!

A pictogram is a simple visual image that represents an object, word or concept. Its meaning is universal and immediate. Olympic Games pictograms were first used at the 1948 games in London. They were used to communicate with visitors from many different countries, appearing on posters, tickets, etc. Today, each sport and discipline has its own pictogram.

Approach

1 **Pictograms:** make a collection of everyday pictograms (e.g. road signs). Ask children what each image means and discuss its use. Show examples of different pictograms from different Olympic Games. Each sport should be easy to identify. Ask children which they prefer and compare styles.

2 Graphic artist Otl Aicher designed one of the most highly regarded sets of pictograms for the 1972 Munich Games. He developed his designs on a geometric diagonal grid. Show examples.

3 Give children sheets of diagonal squared paper. Let them choose a sport and experiment drawing different designs for their own pictogram.

4 Transfer designs to sheets of foam, cut out pictograms and stick onto a background of a different colour. Display all pictograms together in a block.

5 **Posters:** use a digital camera to take a photo of the pictograms and upload this onto the computer. Use photo-editing software to change the colours. You could even make them black and white: children find it especially exciting to experiment with different effects. Print out a range of posters based on the original images.

Resources

- Examples of everyday pictograms
- Grid paper, with diagonal squares
- Pencils
- Sheets of foam, two different colours per child
- Scissors
- PVA glue
- Plain paper bags from craft shops or internet
- Paint, brushes
- Silk screen equipment (optional)
- Digital camera and computer

6 **Paper bags:** children can transfer their designs onto bags using poster paint.

7 **Screen printing:** you could extend the project by showing children how to use their pictogram as a design motif for silk screen printing. You could use this method to print tee shirts or cloth bags.

Cross-curricular links

P.S.H.E.: design pictograms for safety at school.

Maths: ask the children to look at Olympic records and chart records over time in their favourite sports. Ask them to make a graph to show how they have changed. Why might this be?

Paralympic Stamps

The Olympic Games celebrates sporting achievements of all kinds. After World War II, Stoke Mandeville Hospital organised a competition for disabled ex-soldiers to coincide with the 1948 Olympics. The first Paralympics was held in 1960, and today it includes many thousands of athletes.

Show children Royal Mail stamps issued to mark the 2012 Olympic Games, featuring events from both Olympic and Paralympics programmes. Talk about which media were used to create the 30 stamps, each created by a different designer.

Approach

1 **Paralympic stamps:** explain that you are 'commissioning' the class to design stamps for the Paralympic Games and each child should choose a sport. Show children images of their sports.

2 **Marbling:** this technique is especially suited to water sports. Encourage children to sketch their designs on cartridge paper and colour in wax pastels.

3 Demonstrate how to create swirls by dropping marbling ink into water and 'combing' it in circular movements. Invite each child to put their wax picture on top of the ink.

4 Lift out swiftly and hang up to dry. Back on white paper and make scalloped edges with a circular template to imitate perforations. Display as a block on backing paper.

Resources

- Examples of Olympic stamps
- Images of chosen sports
- Cartridge paper, pencils
- Wax pastels
- Marbling ink, tray of water
- Poly tiles and printing equipment
- White and black paper

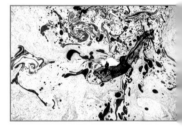

5 **Printing:** ask children to sketch out a design for a Paralympic sport and print this design using poly tiles. Display.

6 Photograph each design and display as a sheet of Olympic stamps.

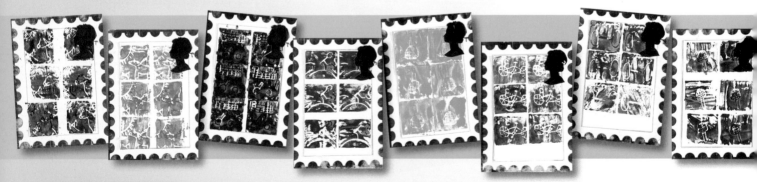

Cross-curricular links

Literacy: research the life story of Ellie Simmonds, Paralympic swimmer.

Design and Technology: research Mandeville, the Paralympics mascot, and design a mascot for your school.

On Wheels

Since the first Olympic Games in Athens, 1896, cycle events have featured in the Olympic programme. Show children how the wheel can also make a decorative device.

Resources
- Images of bicycle wheels and a real bicycle if possible
- Wire, wire cutters (supervised use only)
- White and black paper, card
- Silver paper
- Pencils, paint, brushes
- Straws
- Crepe paper

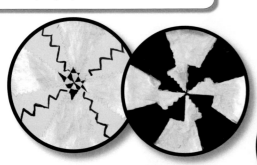

Approach

1   Collect images of bicycles. Discuss how they have changed over the years as technology has advanced. Look at the designs of wheels. Most bicycle wheels use spokes in their designs and there has been much debate over which spoke patterns create the strongest wheels.

2   Encourage children to experiment on paper with different, decorative spoke designs.

3   Demonstrate how to mould a piece of wire into a circle and cover in crepe paper. Create a spoke design by twisting pieces of wire across the frame. Add 'hubs' in silver paper. Display on a giant circle of black paper and decorate with straws as extra 'spokes'. Mount on silver paper.

4   Make extra wheels out of circular paper, painted with children's own designs. Add to the display.

Cross-curricular links

Literacy: research the new 'Omnium' cycling event. Invent a new cycling event and prepare a presentation to the IOC.

Science: look at the history of bicycles and discuss the advances in science and technology.

Inspired by David Hockney

The modern Olympic swimming event has developed a great deal since it began in 1896. There were then three swimming races for men only, which took place in the Mediterranean Sea. There was also a special event open for sailors only. Women first swam in the Olympics in 1912 at Stockholm and swimming has featured at every Paralympic Games since 1960.

Resources

- Images of Hockney swimming pools/ photomontage
- Pencils/paint/brushes/paper
- Sequins, coloured wool, etc.
- Cotton fabric cut into circles
- Dried peas
- Blue dye/elastic bands/ PVA glue
- Crayons
- Photos of swimming pool

Approach

1   Look at the work of English artist David Hockney, explaining that he created a series of paintings of swimming pools. He is also famous for experimenting with different techniques, such as photomontage. Show examples.

2   **Swimming pool pattern:** ask the children to create a swirling swimming pool pattern by taking a line for a walk on a large piece of cartridge paper. Paint in different shades of blue and decorate with sequins and coloured wool, etc.

3   **Tie-die 3D bubbles:** give each child a cotton circle, put dried peas in the centre of the fabric and secure with elastic bands. Place in a bucket of dye, leave for an hour, rinse, dry, and untie the circles. Outline in blue and stick onto the display.

Cross-curricular links

Geography: look at other water sports both in the summer and winter Olympics. Research what conditions/water features would be needed to host these sports.

Inspired by Matisse

Gymnastics have featured in every Olympic Games since 1896 but until 1928 they were for men only. The word gymnastics derives from 'gymnos', a Greek word that means naked. In the original Olympics men would perform without any clothes on. There are two categories, Artistic – including work on beams and vaults – and Rhythmic – where women perform dance routines to music using hoops, ropes, balls and ribbons. The children can research famous gymnasts, e.g. Beth Tweddle, Olga Korbut and Nadia Comaneci.

Resources
- Film of gymnasts
- Coloured paper
- Scissors/PVA glue
- Sticky-backed plastic/fabric
- Pencils/paint/brushes

Approach

1. Show children film of gymnasts and discuss the shapes they make with their bodies. With the correct safety precautions, challenge some children to demonstrate the essence of rhythmic gymnastics. The rest of the class should sketch their poses and movements. Point out the curvature of the body and where weight is focused.

2. Matisse often used music and dance as inspiration. Show pictures of Matisse's cut-out pictures, made from brightly coloured paper. Discuss how the shapes have been simplified and how a few flowing lines portray movement and rhythm.

3. Allow children to experiment with turning their sketches into Matisse-style gymnastic cut-outs, using the five bold colours of the Olympic logo. Add shapes to represent the apparatus that gymnasts use.

4. **Fabric stencil picture:** sketch out a simple outline of a gymnastic shape and transfer it onto the paper backing of the sticky-backed plastic. Demonstrate how to cut out the stencil. Peel off the backing and stick onto a piece of fabric. Paint the background. Allow to dry and peel off the stencil.

Cross-curricular links

P.E.: mark out a 12m × 12m square and put down mats for safety. Watch some Olympic floor gymnastics and ask children to choreograph and perform a simple routine, set to music and with props such as ropes, balls, hoops and ribbons.

Olympic Ball Sports

Olympic ball sports include a wide variety of events from football to table tennis and beach volleyball. Croquet made a one and only appearance at the 1900 Paris Olympics. Show the children images of different Olympic ball events, including ones now dropped from the programme. Research the different types of balls used, their designs and sizes.

Resources
- Standard black and white football
- Black paper
- Hexagonal pieces of white card (or felt/foam)
- Black and white paint, brushes
- Black felt-tip pens
- Circular white card (larger and smaller)
  - Scissors and PVA glue
  - Collage materials

Approach

1   **Football display:** look at a football carefully. It is is made up of lots of different pentagons and hexagons in black and white. Now look at a selection of different shapes – triangles, circles, squares and spirals. Discuss how they could fit into a hexagon.

2   Give each child a hexagonal piece of card and ask them to design a pattern of shapes on it in black and white. They can use collage, paint, felt-tip pen.

3   Draw and cut out large hexagons on black paper and mount on a display board. Fit and stick the hexagonal pieces inside large circles of white card, trimming the hexagons where necessary to make giant 'footballs'.

4   You can also make up some traditional footballs with white hexagons and black pentagons and display these in contrast to the designer balls.

Making a Handball

Handball is arguably one of the fastest ball games around. There are seven players on each side with each team aiming to score the highest number of goals by passing and dribbling the ball.

Approach

1   Cut out circles of coloured paper. Using flat trays of liquid paint, children make handprints around the circles. Remind the children to wash their hands after each colour!

2   Using their own hands as templates, children can draw and cut out hand shapes and paint or crayon and decorate as they choose. Glue onto the circles.

3   Mount on backing paper and display.

Resources

- Images of Olympic ball events
- Coloured and white paper
- Scissors
- Coloured paint, trays
- Brushes, wax crayons, felt-tips
- PVA glue
- Sponge and water for washing hands

Cross-curricular links

Science: which balls bounce best? Research the properties of materials used.

P.E.: play a game of handball.

Literacy: recount a trip to a football match or watching a favourite sport.

Sailing

Sailing is one of the oldest Olympic sports, appearing first in Paris in 1900. Encourage the children to look at the advances in boat design and materials over the years.

Resources
- Images of sailing boats
- Computer and digital camera
- Cartridge paper, ink, felt-tips
- PVA glue

Approach

1 Look at images of sailing boats and discuss their design, especially the brightly coloured spinnakers.

2 Take digital photos of sailing boats on the sea and use photo-editing software to create line drawings from the photos. Print off the images.

3 Children should colour the line drawings with their own designs using felt-tips, collecting them in a collage picture.

3D Sailing Boat

Approach

1 Look at pictures of sailing boats and discuss their shape. Soak willow canes in water.

2 Demonstrate how to bend the canes into the shape of a boat and secure with masking tape. Mix PVA glue and water in a bowl and cover a sheet of tissue paper with the mixture, using a sponge. Drape tissue over the willow frame and cover with another layer of the mixture. Don't forget to add a 'mast'. Allow to dry.

3 Paint with coloured inks.

4 Each child designs and makes a face out of coloured foam and sticks it to the sailing boat. Design, colour and cut out sails from card and attach to the mast with glue.

Resources
- Model boats
- Willow canes
- PVA glue
- Masking tape
- Coloured inks
- Tissue paper, paint brushes
- Coloured foam
- Card
- Sponge

Cross-curricular links

Geography: look at the points of the compass. How do sailors find their way at sea?

Literacy: Write a sailor's log during a long distance solo race.

History: research a country's seafaring past from earliest times.

Track Events and Spectators

The Olympic Games has always inspired art. Host countries have commissioned public art ranging from underpass designs, bridges and security fences, to planting schemes and entrance mats to welcome visitors.

The 2012 Olympics is no exception, and this art is a lasting legacy of the Games.

Resources
- Images of public art
- Black and white paper, pencils
- Scissors
- Large sheet of card
- PVA glue

Approach

1 Talk to children about public art, and research images from all over the world. Ask children to imagine they have been commissioned to create a mural on the walls of the Olympic park, celebrating not only the track events but the spectators too.

2 Ask each child to draw a face. Demonstrate how to draw an oval shape and divide it vertically down the centre. Draw a horizontal line roughly half way across the oval: this is the eye line. The bottom section of the oval can be divided again in half to provide the nose position and finally the remaining section divided once more for the position of the mouth. Explain to the children that this is a rough guide to drawing a face and that everyone's face is different and needs careful observation to recreate the character of the sitter.

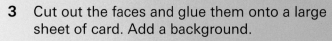

3 Cut out the faces and glue them onto a large sheet of card. Add a background.

4 Draw round a child in running pose on black paper and cut out. Position the runner as a silhouette on the track scene with the 'spectators'.

Cross-curricular links

Literacy: 'Winning words' is a programme of permanent poetry positioned throughout the Olympic park in London. Write a short poem for the Olympics and 'carve' it into a clay tile.

Running Shoes

A lot of Olympic sports require specialised shoes.
Discuss the children's ideas about the types of shoes
that may be used for different sports.

Approach

1 Show children
different designs
for a variety of
running shoes and
discuss the different
materials and
fastenings used.

2 Ask the children to
design a running
shoe for the Olympic
track events.

3 Colour and cut
out the shoes
and assemble
them in a
display.

Resources

- Images and
  designs for
  running shoes
- Card or a
  template of a
  running shoe
- Paint and
  brushes,
  crayons and
  felt-tips

Cross-curricular links

P.S.H.E.: What does it take to set a personal best and how do you beat it?